GREAT
CHICKEN
DISHES

Consultant Editor:
Valerie Ferguson

HERMES
HOUSE

Contents

Introduction

Chicken is popular with almost everyone. It is tender and delicious and adapts beautifully to many cooking methods and flavourings: distinctive recipes for classic chicken dishes abound all over the world. Low in fat and quick to cook, it is equally suitable for everyday meals or sumptuous dinner-party dishes.

Chicken is available whole, quartered or jointed into thighs, drumsticks, breasts and wings. Boneless, skinless portions make preparation very easy. If you prefer not to pay a premium price for individual portions, it is cheaper to buy a whole chicken and joint it yourself, and cheaper still to buy a frozen chicken. Defrost it thoroughly before use, allowing it to thaw slowly in a cool place overnight. Make the most of a whole bird by turning the bones into flavourful stock.

Choose free-range or cornfed birds for the best flavour. Many types of chicken are now available, some with added herbs and other flavourings. Self-basting chickens have butter or olive oil injected into the flesh to keep it moist when roasted. A medium chicken will be enough for four people but baby chickens, called poussins, can be bought to serve whole or halved, depending on their size.

Cuts of Chicken

Chicken pieces are packaged in a variety of ways, and some cuts are available on or off the bone, with or without skin. Some cooking methods are especially suited to specific cuts of meat.

SKINLESS BONELESS THIGH
This makes tasks such as stuffing and rolling much quicker, as it is already skinned and jointed.

LIVER
This makes a wonderful addition to pâtés or salads.

MINCED CHICKEN
Use minced chicken for delicately flavoured stuffings, meatballs, pie fillings and terrines.

DRUMSTICK
The drumstick is a firm favourite for barbecuing or frying, either in batter or rolled in breadcrumbs.

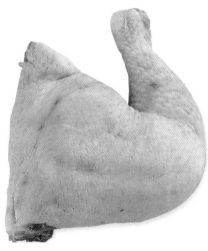

BREAST
Tender white
breast meat cooks
quickly and is best
grilled or fried in butter.

THIGH
The thigh is suitable for casseroling
and other slow-cooking methods.

WING
The wing does not supply much meat,
and is often barbecued or fried.

LEG
The thigh and drumstick together
make up the leg. Large pieces with
bones, like this, are suitable for
slow-cooking, such as casseroling
or poaching.

COOK'S TIP: Large packages of
chicken pieces are an economical
buy; simply use what you need and
freeze the rest. Look out for
individually wrapped joints sold for
this purpose.

Techniques

ROASTING A CHICKEN

Roast chicken is a universal favourite. Start with a good quality chicken which will be full of flavour, season it simply and baste well for perfect crisp skin and moist, delicious meat. To test whether the bird is cooked, stick a skewer into the thickest part of the thigh: the juices that run out should be clear.

1 Wipe the bird inside and out with damp paper towels. Flavourings such as herbs, a clove of garlic or half a lemon may be pushed into the body cavity. Spread the breast with softened butter or oil and tie the legs together.

3 Transfer the bird to a carving board and leave to rest for 15 minutes. To make gravy, skim the fat from the juices in the tin then blend in 15 ml/ 1 tbsp flour. Add 300 ml/½ pint/1 ¼ cups chicken stock and bring to the boil, stirring, to thicken. Season to taste and strain into a jug to serve.

2 Set the chicken breast up on a rack over a roasting tin. Roast, basting every 10 minutes after the first 30 minutes with the accumulated juices and fat in the tin. Cover loosely with foil if it is browning too quickly.

Roasting Times
Poussin
450–700 g/1–1½ lb
1¼ hours at 180°C/350°F/Gas 4
Chicken
1.2–1.3 kg/2½–3 lb
1–1¼ hours at 190°C/375°F/Gas 5
1.5–1.75 kg/3½–4 lb
1¼–1¾ hours at 190°C/375°F/Gas 5
2–2.25 kg/4½–5 lb
1½–2 hours at 190°C/375°F/Gas 5
2.25–2.7 kg/5–6 lb
1¾–2½ hours at 190°C/375°F/Gas 5

CARVING A CHICKEN

It is best to allow the chicken to stand for 10–15 minutes before carving (while the gravy is being made). This allows the meat to relax so that the flesh will not tear during carving. Use a sharp carving knife and work on a plate that will catch any juices – these can be added to the gravy. The leg can be cut into two portions, a thigh and a drumstick.

1 Hold the chicken firmly with a carving fork, between the breast and leg, down to the backbone. Cut the skin around the opposite leg, press gently outwards to expose the ball-and-socket joint and cut through. Slip the knife under the back to remove the "oyster" with the leg.

2 With the knife at the top end of the breastbone, cut down parallel to one side of the wishbone to take a good slice of breast with the wing.

3 With the knife at the end of the breastbone, cut down the front of the carcass, removing the wishbone. Carve the remaining breast into slices.

COOK'S TIP: To make stock, put the carcass from a cooked chicken into a pan with a quartered onion, a carrot, bouquet garni (bay leaf, thyme and parsley) and a few peppercorns. Do not add salt as the seasoning may be too strong when the liquid has reduced. Just cover with cold water, bring to the boil and simmer gently for about 2 hours, removing any scum that rises to the surface with a slotted spoon. Strain the stock into a bowl and leave to cool. When the stock has set, the fat can be scraped off the surface using a spoon.

Indonesian-style Satay Chicken

You do not have to use chicken breast fillet for satays; boneless thighs will give a good flavour and are very economical.

Serves 4

INGREDIENTS
50 g/2 oz/½ cup raw peanuts
45 ml/3 tbsp vegetable oil
1 small onion, finely chopped
2.5 cm/1 in piece root ginger, peeled
    and finely chopped
1 clove garlic, crushed
675 g/1½ lb chicken thighs, skinned
    and cut into cubes
90 g/3½ oz creamed coconut,
    roughly chopped
15 ml/1 tbsp chilli sauce
60 ml/4 tbsp crunchy peanut butter
5 ml/1 tsp soft dark brown sugar
150 ml/¼ pint/⅔ cup milk
1.5 ml/¼ tsp salt

1 Shell and rub the skins from the peanuts, then soak them in enough water to cover for 1 minute. Drain the nuts and cut them into slivers.

2 Heat a wok or heavy-based frying pan and add 5 ml/1 tsp oil. When the oil is hot, stir-fry the peanuts for 1 minute, until crisp and golden. Remove with a slotted spoon and drain on kitchen paper.

3 Add the remaining oil to the wok or pan. When the oil is hot, add the onion, ginger and garlic and stir-fry for 2–3 minutes, until softened but not browned. Remove with a slotted spoon and drain on kitchen paper.

4 Add the chicken pieces and stir-fry for 3–4 minutes until crisp and golden on all sides. Thread on to pre-soaked bamboo skewers and keep warm. Add the creamed coconut to the hot wok in small pieces and stir-fry until melted.

5 Add the chilli sauce, peanut butter and onion mixture, and simmer for 2 minutes. Stir in the sugar, milk and salt, and simmer for a further 3 minutes. Serve the skewered chicken hot, with a dish of the hot dipping sauce sprinkled with the roasted peanuts.

COOK'S TIP: Soak bamboo skewers in cold water for at least 2 hours, or preferably overnight. This will prevent them from charring while the threaded chicken is being kept warm in the oven.

Chicken Cigars

These small, crispy rolls can be served warm as canapés or as a first course with a crisp, colourful salad.

Serves 4

INGREDIENTS
1 x 275 g/10 oz packet of filo pastry
45 ml/3 tbsp olive oil
fresh parsley, to garnish

FOR THE FILLING
350 g/12 oz minced raw chicken
1 egg, beaten
2.5 ml/½ tsp ground cinnamon
2.5 ml/½ tsp ground ginger
30 ml/2 tbsp raisins
15 ml/1 tbsp olive oil
1 small onion, finely chopped
salt and freshly ground
    black pepper

1 Mix all the filling ingredients, except the oil and onion, together in a bowl. Heat the oil in a large frying pan and cook the onion until tender. Leave to cool, then add to the remaining mixed ingredients.

2 Preheat the oven to 180°C/350°F/ Gas 4 and prepare the filo pastry. Once the packet has been opened, keep the pastry covered with a damp tea towel and work fast, as it dries out very quickly when exposed to the air. Unravel the pastry and cut into 10 x 25 cm/4 x 10 in strips.

3 Covering the remaining strips, take a single strip of pastry, brush with a little olive oil and place a small spoonful of the filling about 1 cm/ ½ in from the end.

4 To encase the filling, fold the long sides inwards to a width of 5 cm/ 2 in and roll along the length into a cigar shape. Place on a greased baking tray and brush with olive oil. Bake the cigars for about 20–25 minutes, until golden brown and crisp. Garnish with sprigs of fresh parsley.

Brandied Chicken Liver Pâté

The rich flavour of chicken livers in this delicious starter is enhanced by the addition of a little brandy.

Serves 4–6

INGREDIENTS
350 g/12 oz chicken livers
115 g/4 oz/½ cup butter
1 slice rindless streaky bacon,
    chopped
1 shallot, chopped
2 garlic cloves, crushed
30 ml/2 tbsp brandy
30 ml/2 tbsp chopped fresh parsley
salt and freshly ground black pepper
fresh bay leaves and peppercorns,
    to garnish
olive bread, to serve
radishes, to serve (optional)

2 Stir in the brandy and chopped parsley, with salt and pepper to taste. Bring to the boil and cook for about 2 minutes, then remove from the heat and process in a blender or food processor until smooth.

3 Spoon the pâté into individual serving dishes. Melt the remaining butter and pour it carefully over the surface of each dish of pâté to form a seal. Garnish with fresh bay leaves and peppercorns.

4 When cool, chill the pâté until firm. Serve with olive bread and a few radishes, if liked.

1 Rinse, trim and roughly chop the chicken livers. Melt half the butter in a large frying pan. Add the bacon, shallot and garlic and fry for 5 minutes. Add the chicken livers and fry gently for a further 5 minutes.

COOK'S TIP: If properly sealed, the pâté will keep in the fridge for 3–4 days.

Chicken & Vegetable Soup

A thick, chunky chicken and vegetable soup served with garlic-flavoured fried croûtons is a meal in itself.

Serves 4

INGREDIENTS
4 boneless, skinless chicken thighs
15 g/½ oz/1 tbsp butter
2 small leeks, thinly sliced
25 g/1 oz/2 tbsp long grain rice
900 ml/1½ pints/3¾ cups chicken stock
15 ml/1 tbsp chopped mixed fresh parsley
   and mint
salt and freshly ground black pepper

FOR THE GARLIC CROÛTONS
30 ml/2 tbsp olive oil
1 garlic clove, crushed
4 slices of bread, cut into cubes

1 Cut the chicken into 1 cm/½ in cubes. Melt the butter in a saucepan, add the leeks and cook until tender. Add the rice and chicken and cook for a further 2 minutes.

2 Add the stock, then cover and simmer for 15–20 minutes, until the chicken is tender.

3 To make the garlic croûtons, heat the oil in a large frying pan. Add the garlic and bread cubes and cook, stirring constantly, until golden brown. Drain on kitchen paper and sprinkle with a pinch of salt.

4 Add the chopped parsley and mint mixture to the soup and adjust the seasoning according to taste. Serve the soup immediately and hand the garlic croûtons around separately.

Chicken & Buckwheat Noodle Soup

Buckwheat or soba noodles are widely enjoyed in Japan. The simplest way of serving them is in hot seasoned broth.

Serves 4

INGREDIENTS
225 g/8 oz skinless, boneless chicken breasts
120 ml/4 fl oz/½ cup soy sauce
15 ml/1 tbsp saké or dry sherry
1 litre/1¾ pints/4 cups
    chicken stock
2 young leeks, cut into 2.5 cm/1 in pieces
175 g/6 oz spinach leaves
300 g/11 oz buckwheat or
    soba noodles
sesame seeds, toasted,
    to garnish

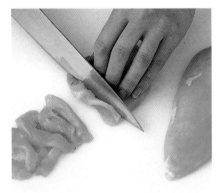

1 Slice the chicken diagonally into bite-size pieces. Combine the soy sauce and saké or sherry in a saucepan. Bring to a simmer. Add the chicken and cook gently for about 3 minutes, until it is tender. Keep hot.

2 Bring the chicken stock to the boil in a saucepan. Add the leeks and simmer for 3 minutes, then add the spinach and cook until it is just wilted. Remove from the heat, but cover to keep warm.

3 Cook the buckwheat or soba noodles for about 5 minutes in a large saucepan of gently boiling water until just tender, following the packet instructions.

4 Drain the cooked noodles and divide them among individual serving bowls. Ladle the hot leek and spinach broth into the bowls, then add a portion of hot chicken to each. Serve the soup at once, sprinkled with toasted sesame seeds.

Thai-style Chicken Soup

A fragrant blend of coconut milk, lemon grass, ginger and lime makes a delicious soup, with just a hint of chilli.

Serves 4

INGREDIENTS
5 ml/1 tsp oil
1–2 fresh red chillies, seeded and chopped
2 garlic cloves, crushed
1 large leek, thinly sliced
600 ml/1 pint/2½ cups chicken stock
400 ml/14 fl oz/1⅔ cups coconut milk
450 g/1 lb boneless, skinless chicken thighs
30 ml/2 tbsp Thai fish sauce
1 lemon grass stick, split
2.5 cm/1 in piece fresh root ginger, peeled and finely chopped
5 ml/1 tsp sugar
3 kaffir lime leaves (optional)
75 g/3 oz/¾ cup frozen peas, thawed
45 ml/3 tbsp chopped fresh coriander

1 Heat the oil in a large saucepan and cook the chillies and garlic for about 2 minutes. Add the leek and cook for a further 2 minutes. Stir in the stock and coconut milk and bring to the boil.

2 Cut the chicken into bite-size pieces and add to the pan with the fish sauce, lemon grass, ginger, sugar and lime leaves, if using. Cover and simmer, stirring occasionally, for 15 minutes, or until the chicken is tender.

3 Add the peas and cook for a further 3 minutes. Remove the lemon grass and stir in the coriander just before serving.

Chicken Mulligatawny

This is a popular variation of mulligatawny – pepper water – which was originally a spiced vegetable soup with a distinctive sour flavour.

Serves 4–6

INGREDIENTS
900 g/2 lb diced chicken
6 green cardamom pods
1 piece cinnamon stick, 5 cm/2 in long
4–6 curry leaves
15 ml/1 tbsp coriander powder
5 ml/1 tsp cumin powder
2.5 ml/½ tsp turmeric
3 cloves garlic, crushed
salt and 12 black peppercorns
4 cloves
1 onion, finely chopped
115 g/4 oz coconut cream block
juice of 2 lemons
deep-fried onions, to garnish
chopped coriander leaves, to garnish

1 Place the chicken in a large pan with 575 ml/1 pint/2½ cups water and cook until the chicken is tender. Skim the surface, then strain, reserving the stock and keeping the chicken warm.

2 Return the stock to the pan and reheat. Add all the remaining ingredients, except the chicken, deep-fried onions and coriander. Simmer for 10–15 minutes.

3 Strain the mixture and return the cooked chicken to the soup. Reheat and serve in individual bowls, garnished with deep-fried onions and chopped coriander.

Roasted Chicken with Mediterranean Vegetables

This is a delicious French alternative to a traditional roast chicken. Use a cornfed or free-range bird, if available.

Serves 4

INGREDIENTS
1.75 kg/4–4½ lb roasting chicken
150 ml/¼ pint/⅔ cup extra virgin
    olive oil
½ lemon
few sprigs of fresh thyme
450 g/1 lb small new potatoes
1 aubergine, cut into 2.5 cm/1 in cubes
1 red pepper, seeded and quartered
1 fennel bulb, trimmed and quartered
8 large garlic cloves,
    unpeeled
coarse salt and freshly ground
    black pepper

1 Preheat the oven to 200°C/400°F/ Gas 6. Rub the chicken all over with olive oil and season with pepper. Place the lemon half inside the bird, with a sprig or two of fresh thyme. Put the chicken, breast side down, in a large roasting tin. Roast for about 30 minutes.

2 Remove the chicken from the oven and season with salt. Turn the chicken right side up and baste with the juices from the tin. Surround the bird with the potatoes, roll them in the cooking juices, and return the roasting tin to the oven.

3 After 30 minutes, add the aubergine, red pepper, fennel and garlic cloves to the tin. Drizzle with the remaining oil and season with salt and pepper. Add any remaining thyme to the vegetables. Return to the oven, and cook for a further 30–50 minutes, basting and turning the vegetables occasionally.

4 To check if the chicken is cooked, push the tip of a sharp knife between the thigh and breast. If the juices run clear, it is done. The vegetables should be tender and just beginning to brown. Serve the chicken and vegetables from the tin, or transfer the vegetables to a serving dish, joint the chicken, and place it on top. Serve the skimmed juices in a gravy boat.

Chicken Casserole

A casserole of wonderfully tender chicken, root vegetables and lentils, finished with crème fraîche, mustard and tarragon.

Serves 4

INGREDIENTS
350 g/12 oz onions
350 g/12 oz trimmed leeks
225 g/8 oz carrots
450 g/1 lb swede
30 ml/2 tbsp oil
4 chicken portions, about 900 g/2 lb total
    weight
115 g/4 oz/½ cup green lentils
475 ml/16 fl oz/2 cups chicken stock
300 ml/½ pint/1¼ cups apple juice
10 ml/2 tsp cornflour
30 ml/2 tbsp water
45ml/3 tbsp crème fraîche
10 ml/2 tsp wholegrain mustard
30 ml/2 tbsp chopped fresh tarragon
salt and freshly ground black pepper
fresh tarragon sprigs, to garnish

1 Preheat the oven to 190°C/375°F/ Gas 5. Prepare the onions, leeks, carrots and swede and roughly chop into pieces of a similar size.

2 Heat the oil in a large flameproof casserole. Season the chicken portions with salt and pepper and brown them in the hot oil until golden. Drain on kitchen paper.

3 Add the onions to the casserole and cook, stirring, for 5 minutes, until they begin to soften and colour.

4 Stir in the leeks, carrots, swede and lentils and stir over a medium heat for 2 minutes.

5 Return the chicken to the pan. Add the stock, apple juice and seasoning. Bring to the boil and cover tightly. Cook in the oven for 50–60 minutes, or until the chicken and lentils are tender.

6 Place the casserole over a medium heat. Blend the cornflour and water and add with the crème fraîche, mustard and tarragon. Adjust seasoning. Simmer for about 2 minutes, stirring. Serve garnished with tarragon sprigs.

Chicken & Leek Parcels

These intriguing parcels may sound a bit fiddly, but they take very little time and you can freeze them.

Serves 4

INGREDIENTS
4 chicken fillets or boneless
    breast portions
2 small leeks, sliced
2 carrots, grated
4 stoned black olives, chopped
1 garlic clove, crushed
15–30 ml/1–2 tbsp olive oil
8 anchovy fillets
salt and freshly ground black pepper
black olives and herb sprigs, to garnish

1 Preheat the oven to 200°C/400°F/ Gas 6. Season the chicken well. Divide the leeks equally among four sheets of greased greaseproof paper, about 23 cm/9 in square. Place a piece of chicken on top of each portion.

2 Mix the carrots, olives, garlic and oil together. Season lightly and place on top of the chicken portions. Top each with two anchovy fillets, then carefully wrap up each parcel, making sure the folds are underneath and the carrot mixture on top.

3 Bake for 20 minutes and serve hot, in the paper, garnished with black olives and herb sprigs.

Chicken in a Tomato Coat

This dish has a delicious summery flavour and would make a wonderful al fresco supper.

Serves 4–6

INGREDIENTS
1.5–1.75 kg/3½–4 lb free-range chicken
1 small onion
knob of butter
75 ml/5 tbsp ready-made tomato sauce
30 ml/2 tbsp chopped, mixed fresh herbs,
    such as parsley, tarragon, sage, basil and
    marjoram, or 10 ml/2 tsp dried
small glass of dry white wine
2–3 small tomatoes, sliced
olive oil
little cornflour (optional)
salt and freshly ground
    black pepper

1 Preheat the oven to 190°C/375°F/ Gas 5. Place the onion, butter and seasoning inside the cleaned chicken and put in a roasting tin. Cover with most of the tomato sauce, half the herbs and more seasoning. Pour in the wine.

2 Cover with foil and roast for 1½ hours, basting occasionally. Spread with the rest of the sauce, tomatoes and oil and cook for 20–30 minutes more. Sprinkle with remaining herbs and carve. Thicken sauce with cornflour if liked. Serve hot.

Chicken Pie with Mushrooms

The filling in this pie has an intense mushroom flavour, using chicken stock rather than the more usual milk and butter.

Serves 4–6

INGREDIENTS
FOR THE PASTRY
150 g/5 oz/scant ¾ cup butter or
    margarine, chilled
225 g/8 oz/2 cups plain flour
1 egg yolk
60 ml/4 tbsp cold water

FOR THE PIE FILLING
900 g/2 lb cooked roast or boiled chicken
45 ml/3 tbsp olive oil
275 g/10 oz mixed dark mushrooms
    (flat, oyster or chestnut), thickly sliced
25 ml/5 tsp flour
300 ml/½ pint/1¼ cups chicken stock
15 ml/1 tbsp soy sauce
1 egg white
salt and freshly ground
    black pepper

1 For the pastry, cut the butter or margarine into small pieces and rub it into the flour until it resembles breadcrumbs. Mix the egg yolk with the cold water and stir it into the flour mixture. Form the dough into a ball, cover and chill for about 30 minutes.

2 Preheat the oven to 220°C/425°F/ Gas 7. For the filling, cut the cooked chicken into pieces and put them in a greased pie dish about 1.75 litres/3 pints/7½ cups capacity.

3 Heat half the oil in a frying pan. Sauté the mushrooms over a high heat for about 3 minutes. Add the remaining oil and stir in the flour. Season with pepper and slowly add the stock, stirring to make a thick sauce.

4 Stir in the soy sauce, taste for seasoning and pour the mushroom sauce over the chicken.

5 Roll out the pastry and cut one piece slightly larger than the size of the pie dish. Also cut some long strips about 2 cm/¾ in wide. Place these around the rim of the pie dish, then lift the large pastry piece on to the top, pressing it down on top of the strips. Knock up the edges with a knife.

6 Lightly whisk the egg white with a fork and brush it over the pastry to ensure a golden and crisp finish. Bake the pie in the preheated oven for about 30–35 minutes. Serve immediately.

COOK'S TIP: The pie can be made in advance up to Step 4 and chilled overnight or frozen. To cook from frozen, leave at room temperature for a few hours and cook as above.

Chicken & Prawn Jambalaya

Jambalayas are a colourful mixture of highly flavoured ingredients, and are always made in large quantities for big family or celebration meals.

Serves 10

INGREDIENTS
2 x 1.5 kg/3–3½ lb chickens
450 g/1 lb piece raw smoked gammon
50 g/2 oz/4 tbsp lard or bacon fat
50 g/2 oz/½ cup plain flour
3 medium onions, finely sliced
2 sweet green peppers, seeded and sliced
675 g/1½ lb tomatoes, peeled and chopped
2–3 garlic cloves, crushed
10 ml/2 tsp chopped fresh thyme or 5 ml/
   1 tsp dried thyme
24 Mediterranean prawns, peeled
500 g/1¼ lb/4 cups American long-grain rice
2–3 dashes Tabasco sauce
1 bunch spring onions, finely chopped
45 ml/3 tbsp chopped fresh parsley
salt and freshly ground black pepper

1 Cut each chicken into 10 pieces and season with salt and pepper. Dice the gammon, discarding the rind and fat.

2 In a large heavy-based pan, melt the lard or bacon fat and brown the chicken pieces all over, lifting them out with a slotted spoon and setting them aside as they are done.

3 Lower the heat, sprinkle the flour on to the fat in the pan and stir continuously until the roux turns light golden brown.

4 Return the chicken pieces to the pan, add the gammon, onions, green peppers, peeled tomatoes, garlic and thyme and cook, stirring regularly, for 10 minutes, then stir in the peeled prawns, mixing well.

5 Stir the rice into the pan with one and a half times the rice's volume in cold water. Season with salt, pepper and Tabasco sauce.

6 Bring the mixture to the boil, reduce the heat and cook gently until the rice is tender and the liquid absorbed. Add a little extra boiling water if the rice looks like drying out while it is cooking.

7 Mix the spring onions and parsley into the finished dish, reserving a little of the mixture to scatter over the Jambalaya. Serve hot.

Tandoori Chicken

This is probably the most famous of Indian dishes. Marinate the chicken well and cook in an extremely hot oven for a clay-oven-baked taste.

Serves 4–6

INGREDIENTS
1.3 kg/3 lb ready-to-roast chicken
250 ml/8 fl oz/1 cup natural yogurt, beaten
60 ml/4 tbsp tandoori masala paste
75 g/3 oz ghee
salt
lemon wedges and onion rings, to garnish
lettuce, to serve

1 Using a sharp knife or scissors, remove the skin from the chicken and trim off any excess fat. Using a fork, beat the flesh at random.

2 Cut the chicken in half down the centre and through the breast. Cut each piece in half again. Make a few deep gashes diagonally into the flesh. Mix the yogurt with the masala paste and salt. Spread the chicken evenly with the yogurt mixture, spreading some into the gashes. Leave for at least 2 hours, but preferably overnight.

3 Preheat the oven to its hottest setting. Place the marinated chicken quarters on a wire rack in a deep baking tray. Spread the chicken pieces with any excess marinade, reserving a little for basting halfway through the cooking time.

4 Melt the ghee and pour over the chicken quarters to seal the surface. This helps to keep the centre of the chicken moist during the roasting period. Cook in the oven for 10 minutes at the maximum heat, then remove, leaving the oven switched on.

5 Baste the chicken pieces with the remaining marinade. Return to the oven and switch off the heat. Leave the chicken in the oven for about 15–20 minutes without opening the door. Serve on a bed of lettuce and garnish with the lemon and onion rings.

Glazed Chicken with Cashew Nuts

Hoisin sauce lends a sweet yet slightly hot note to this chicken dish, while cashew nuts add a pleasing contrast of texture.

Serves 4

INGREDIENTS
1 red pepper
450 g/1 lb skinless and boneless
  chicken breasts
75 g/3 oz/¾ cup cashew nuts
45 ml/3 tbsp groundnut oil
4 garlic cloves, finely chopped
30 ml/2 tbsp Chinese rice wine or medium-
  dry sherry
45 ml/3 tbsp hoisin sauce
10 ml/2 tsp sesame oil
5–6 spring onions, green parts only, cut into
  2.5 cm/1 in lengths
rice or noodles, to serve

1 Halve the red pepper and remove the seeds. Slice into finger-length strips. Flatten the chicken breasts and slice into strips of a similar size to the pepper pieces.

2 Heat a wok or heavy-based frying pan until hot, add the cashew nuts and stir-fry over a low to medium heat for 1–2 minutes, until golden brown. Remove and set aside.

3 Increase the heat under the wok or pan, add the oil and swirl around. Add the garlic and let it sizzle for a few seconds. Add the pepper and chicken strips to the pan and stir-fry for 2 minutes.

4 Add the rice wine or sherry and hoisin sauce. Continue to stir-fry until the chicken is tender and all the ingredients are evenly glazed.

5 Stir in the sesame oil, cashew nuts and spring onion tips. Serve immediately with rice or noodles.

Devilled Chicken

You can tell this spicy, barbecued chicken dish comes from southern Italy because it has dried red chillies in the marinade.

Serves 4

INGREDIENTS
120 ml/4 fl oz/½ cup olive oil
finely grated rind and juice of 1 large lemon
2 garlic cloves, finely chopped
10 ml/2 tsp finely chopped or crumbled dried
  red chillies
12 skinless, boneless chicken thighs, each
  cut into 3 or 4 pieces
salt and freshly ground black pepper
flat leaf parsley leaves, to garnish
lemon wedges, to serve

1 Mix the oil, lemon rind and juice, garlic and chillies in a shallow dish. Season to taste. Whisk well.

2 Add the chicken pieces, turning to coat with the marinade. Cover and refrigerate for at least 4 hours.

3 When ready to cook, prepare the barbecue or preheat the grill and thread the chicken pieces on to eight oiled metal skewers. Cook on the barbecue or under a hot grill for 6–8 minutes, turning frequently, until tender. Garnish with parsley leaves and serve hot, with lemon wedges.

COOK'S TIP: Thread the chicken on the skewers spiral-fashion so it does not fall off during cooking.

Spicy Fried Chicken

Tender fried chicken pieces are given a mouth-watering spicy kick with a crisp coating of paprika.

Serves 4

INGREDIENTS
120 ml/4 fl oz/½ cup buttermilk
1.5 kg/3–3½ lb chicken pieces
50 g/2 oz/½ cup plain flour
15 ml/1 tbsp paprika
5 ml/1 tsp freshly ground black pepper
vegetable oil, for frying
15 ml/1 tbsp water

1 Pour the buttermilk into a large bowl and add the chicken pieces. Stir to coat, then set aside for 5 minutes. In a bowl or plastic bag, combine the flour, paprika and freshly ground black pepper.

2 Heat 5 mm/¼ in of oil in a large frying pan over medium-high heat. One by one, lift the chicken pieces out of the buttermilk and dip into the flour to coat, shaking off any excess.

3 Add the chicken pieces to the hot oil and fry for about 10 minutes, until lightly browned, turning once.

4 Reduce the heat and add the water. Cover and cook for 30 minutes, turning the pieces over at 10-minute intervals. Uncover the pan and continue cooking for about 15 minutes, until the chicken is very tender and the coating is crisp.

Spinach Tagliarini with Chicken & Asparagus

The combination of chicken and asparagus gives this delicious pasta dish a delicate and sophisticated flavour.

Serves 4–6

INGREDIENTS

2 skinless, boneless chicken breasts
15 ml/1 tbsp light soy sauce
30 ml/2 tbsp sherry
30 ml/2 tbsp cornflour
8 spring onions, trimmed and cut into
    2.5 cm/1 in diagonal slices
1–2 garlic cloves, crushed
needle shreds of rind of ½ lemon and 30 ml/
    2 tbsp lemon juice
150 ml/¼ pint/⅔ cup chicken stock
5 ml/1 tsp caster sugar
225 g/8 oz slender asparagus spears, cut in
    7.5 cm/3 in lengths
450 g/1 lb fresh tagliarini verde or 250 g/
    9 oz dried tagliarini verde
salt and freshly ground black pepper

2 Cut into 2.5 cm/1 in strips across the grain of the fillets. Put the chicken into a bowl with the soy sauce, sherry, cornflour and seasoning. Toss to coat each piece.

3 In a large non-stick frying pan, put the chicken, spring onions, garlic and lemon rind. Add the stock and bring to the boil, stirring constantly until thickened. Add the sugar, lemon juice and asparagus. Simmer for 4–5 minutes until tender.

4 Meanwhile, cook the tagliarini in a large pan of boiling, salted water for 2–3 minutes, if using fresh, or 10–12 minutes, if using dried. Drain thoroughly. Arrange the tagliarini on serving plates and spoon the chicken and asparagus sauce over the top. Serve immediately.

1 Place the chicken breasts between two sheets of clear film and flatten to a thickness of around 5 mm/¼ in with a rolling-pin.

Smoked Chicken, Yellow Pepper & Sun-dried Tomato Pizzette

The ingredients for this recipe complement each other perfectly and make a really delicious topping for these scrumptious little pizzas.

Serves 4

INGREDIENTS

FOR THE PIZZA DOUGH
175 g/6 oz/1½ cups strong white flour
1.5 ml/¼ tsp salt
5 ml/1 tsp easy-blend yeast
120–150 ml/4–5 fl oz/½–⅔ cup
   lukewarm water
15 ml/1 tbsp olive oil

FOR THE TOPPING
45 ml/3 tbsp olive oil
60 ml/4 tbsp sun-dried tomato paste
2 yellow peppers, seeded and cut into
   thin strips
175 g/6 oz sliced smoked chicken, chopped
150 g/5 oz mozzarella cheese, cubed
30 ml/2 tbsp chopped fresh basil
salt and freshly ground black pepper

1 To make the dough, sift the flour and salt into a bowl and stir in the yeast. Make a well in the centre, pour in the water and oil and mix to a soft dough. Knead the dough for about 10 minutes, until it is smooth and elastic. Place it in a greased bowl, cover with clear film and leave in a warm place for about 1 hour, or until it has doubled in size.

2 Preheat the oven to 220°C/425°F/ Gas 7. Knock back the dough. Turn on to a lightly floured surface and knead again for 2–3 minutes. Divide the dough into four pieces and roll out each one on a lightly floured surface to a 13 cm/5 in circle. Place well apart on two greased baking sheets, then push up the dough edges to make a thin rim.

3 Brush the pizza bases with 15 ml/ 1 tbsp of the oil, then brush generously with the sun-dried tomato paste.

4 Stir-fry the peppers in half the remaining oil for 3–4 minutes. Arrange the chicken and peppers on top of the sun-dried tomato paste.

5 Scatter over the mozzarella cheese and basil. Season with salt and black pepper. Drizzle over the remaining oil and bake for 15–20 minutes until crisp and golden. Serve immediately.

VARIATION: Try roasting or grilling the peppers, removing the skins before using.

Cornfed Chicken Salad

A light first course for eight people or a substantial main course for four.

Serves 8

INGREDIENTS
1 x 1.75 kg/4–4½ lb cornfed chicken
300 ml/½ pint/1¼ cups white wine and
    water, mixed
24 x 5 mm/¼ in slices French bread
1 garlic clove
225 g/8 oz French beans
115 g/4 oz fresh young spinach leaves
2 sticks celery, thinly sliced
2 sun-dried tomatoes, chopped
2 spring onions, thinly sliced
fresh chives and parsley, to garnish

FOR THE VINAIGRETTE
30 ml/2 tbsp red wine vinegar
90 ml/6 tbsp olive oil
15 ml/1 tbsp wholegrain mustard
15 ml/1 tbsp clear honey
30 ml/2 tbsp chopped mixed fresh herbs,
    such as thyme, parsley and chives
10 ml/2 tsp finely chopped capers
salt and freshly ground black pepper

1 Preheat the oven to 190°C/375°F/
Gas 5. Put the chicken into a
casserole with the wine and water.
Roast for 1½ hours until tender. Leave
to cool in the liquid. Remove the skin
and bones and cut into small pieces.

2 To make the vinaigrette, put all
the ingredients into a screw-top
jar and shake vigorously. Adjust the
seasoning to taste.

3 Toast the French bread slices under
the grill or in the oven until they
are dry and golden brown, then
lightly rub each one with the peeled
garlic clove.

4 Trim the French beans, cut into
5 cm/2 in lengths and cook in
boiling water until just tender. Drain
and rinse under cold running water.

5 Wash the spinach, remove the stalks
and tear the leaves into small
pieces. Arrange attractively on
individual serving plates with the
sliced celery, cooked French beans,
sun-dried tomatoes, chicken pieces
and sliced spring onions.

6 Spoon over the vinaigrette
dressing. Arrange the toasted
croûtons on top, garnish with extra
fresh chives and parsley, if desired, and
serve immediately.

Chicken Liver Salad

This salad may be served as a first course on individual plates or, would make a light lunch, served with crusty bread.

Serves 4

INGREDIENTS

mixed salad leaves, e.g. frisée and oakleaf
    lettuce or radicchio
1 avocado, peeled and diced
2 pink grapefruits, segmented
350 g/12 oz chicken livers
30 ml/2 tbsp olive oil
1 garlic clove, crushed
salt and freshly ground black pepper
warm crusty bread,
    to serve

FOR THE DRESSING

30 ml/2 tbsp lemon juice
60 ml/4 tbsp olive oil
2.5 ml/½ tsp wholegrain mustard
2.5 ml/½ tsp clear honey
15 ml/1 tbsp snipped
    fresh chives

1 First prepare the dressing: put all the ingredients into a screw-topped jar and shake vigorously to emulsify. Taste and adjust the seasoning.

2 Wash and dry the salad leaves. Arrange attractively on a serving plate with the avocado and grapefruit.

3 Dry the chicken livers on kitchen paper and remove any unwanted pieces. Cut the larger livers in half and leave the smaller ones whole.

4 Heat the oil in a large frying pan. Stir-fry the livers and garlic briskly until the livers are brown all over (they should be slightly pink inside).

5 Season the livers with salt and freshly ground black pepper and drain on kitchen paper.

6 Place the livers on the salad and spoon over the dressing. Serve immediately with warm crusty bread.

Curried Chicken Salad

This unusual salad is a wonderful combination of crisp beans, fresh
tomatoes, chicken in a spiced, creamy sauce and pasta.

Serves 4

INGREDIENTS
2 cooked chicken breasts, boned
175 g/6 oz French beans
350 g/12 oz dried multi-coloured penne
150 ml/¼ pint/⅔ cup yogurt
5 ml/1 tsp mild curry powder
1 garlic clove, crushed
1 green chilli, seeded and finely chopped
30 ml/2 tbsp chopped fresh coriander
4 firm ripe tomatoes, skinned, seeded and cut
   in strips
salt and freshly ground black pepper
fresh coriander leaves, to garnish

3 To make the sauce, mix the yogurt, curry powder, garlic, chilli and chopped coriander together in a bowl. Stir in the chicken pieces and set aside for 30 minutes.

1 Remove the skin from the chicken and cut in strips. Cut the green beans in 2.5 cm/1 in lengths and cook in boiling water for 5 minutes. Drain and rinse under cold water.

2 Cook the pasta in a large pan of boiling, salted water for 10 minutes, until just tender. Drain and rinse.

4 Transfer the cooked pasta to a large serving bowl and toss with the French beans and the strips of tomato. Spoon the chicken and curried sauce over the top of the pasta. Garnish the dish with fresh coriander leaves and serve as soon as possible.

Egg Noodle Salad with Sesame Chicken

This substantial chicken and noodle salad – with its distinctively Chinese flavour – would make a meal in itself.

Serves 4–6

INGREDIENTS
400 g/14 oz fresh thin egg noodles
1 carrot, cut into long fine strips
50 g/2 oz mangetouts, topped, tailed, cut into fine strips and blanched
115 g/4 oz beansprouts, blanched
30 ml/2 tbsp olive oil
225 g/8 oz skinless, boneless chicken breasts, finely sliced
30 ml/2 tbsp sesame seeds, toasted
2 spring onions, finely sliced diagonally, and coriander leaves, to garnish

FOR THE DRESSING
45 ml/3 tbsp sherry vinegar
75 ml/5 tbsp soy sauce
60 ml/4 tbsp sesame oil
90 ml/6 tbsp light olive oil
1 garlic clove, finely chopped
5 ml/1 tsp grated fresh root ginger
salt and freshly ground black pepper

1 To make the dressing, combine all the ingredients in a small bowl with a pinch of salt and mix together well using a whisk or fork.

2 Cook the noodles in a large saucepan of boiling water. Stir them occasionally to separate. They will only take a few minutes to cook.

3 Drain the noodles, rinse under cold running water and drain well. Tip into a bowl. Add the vegetables to the noodles. Pour in about half the dressing, then toss well and adjust the seasoning to taste.

4 Heat the olive oil in a large frying pan. Add the slices of chicken and stir-fry for 3 minutes, or until cooked and golden. Remove the pan from the heat. Add the toasted sesame seeds and drizzle in some of the remaining dressing.

5 Arrange the noodles in "nests" on individual serving plates. Spoon the stir-fried chicken on top. Sprinkle with the sliced spring onions and coriander leaves and serve any remaining dressing separately.

Maryland Salad

Barbecue-grilled chicken, sweetcorn, bacon, banana and watercress combine here in a sensational main-course salad. Serve with jacket potatoes and a knob of butter.

Serves 4

INGREDIENTS
4 boneless chicken breasts
oil, for brushing
225 g/8 oz rindless unsmoked bacon
4 sweetcorn cobs
45 ml/3 tbsp softened butter
4 ripe bananas, peeled and halved
4 firm tomatoes, halved
1 escarole or butterhead lettuce
1 bunch watercress
salt and freshly ground black pepper

DRESSING
75 ml/5 tbsp groundnut oil
15 ml/1 tbsp white wine vinegar
10 ml/2 tsp maple syrup
10 ml/2 tsp mild mustard

1 Season the chicken breasts, brush with oil and barbecue or grill for 15 minutes, turning once. Barbecue or grill the bacon for 8–10 minutes, or until crisp.

2 Bring a large saucepan of salted water to the boil. Shuck and trim the corn cobs or leave the husks on if you prefer. Boil for 20 minutes. For extra flavour, brush with butter and brown over the barbecue or under the grill. Barbecue or grill the halved bananas and tomatoes for 6–8 minutes: you can brush these with butter too if you wish.

3 To make the dressing, combine the oil, vinegar, maple syrup, mustard and 15 ml/1 tbsp water in a screw-top jar and shake well.

4 Wash the escarole or butterhead lettuce and the watercress. Spin thoroughly and dress.

5 Distribute the salad leaves among 4 large plates. Slice the chicken and arrange over the salad with the bacon, banana, sweetcorn and tomatoes.

Baby Chickens with Lime & Chilli

Poussins are ideal for one to two portions. The best way to cook them is spatchcocked – flattened out – to ensure more even cooking.

Serves 4

INGREDIENTS
4 poussins or Cornish hens, about 450 g/1 lb each
45 ml/3 tbsp butter
30 ml/2 tbsp sun-dried tomato paste
finely grated rind of 1 lime
10 ml/2 tsp chilli sauce
juice of ½ lime
flat leaf parsley sprigs, to garnish
lime wedges, to serve

1 Place each poussin on a board, breast side upwards, and press down firmly with your hand, to break the breastbone.

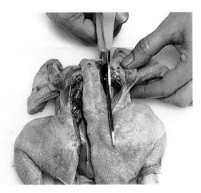

2 Turn the poussin over and, with poultry shears or strong kitchen scissors, cut down either side of the backbone and remove it.

3 Turn each poussin breast-side up and flatten it neatly. Lift the breast skin carefully and gently ease your fingers underneath to loosen it from the flesh.

4 Mix together the butter, tomato paste, lime rind and chilli sauce. Spread evenly under the skin of each poussin, setting aside a quarter of the mixture.

5 To hold the poussins flat during cooking, thread two skewers through each bird, crossing at the centre. Each skewer should pass through a wing and then out through a drumstick on the other side.

6 Mix the reserved paste with the lime juice and brush it over the skin of the poussins. Cook on a medium-hot barbecue or under a preheated grill, turning occasionally, for 25–30 minutes, or until the juices run clear. Garnish with parsley and serve with lime wedges.

COOK'S TIP: If you wish to serve half a poussin per portion, you may find it easier simply to cut the birds in half lengthways using poultry shears or a large sharp knife.

Chicken Roll

The roll can be prepared and cooked the day before and will freeze well too. Remove from the fridge about an hour before serving.

Serves 8

INGREDIENTS
2 kg/4½ lb chicken

FOR THE STUFFING
1 medium onion,
    finely chopped
50 g/2 oz/4 tbsp melted butter
350 g/12 oz lean minced pork
115 g/4 oz streaky bacon,
    chopped
15 ml/1 tbsp chopped fresh parsley
10 ml/2 tsp chopped fresh thyme
115 g/4 oz/2 cups fresh white
    breadcrumbs
30 ml/2 tbsp sherry
1 large egg, beaten
25 g/1 oz/¼ cup shelled pistachio nuts
25 g/1 oz/¼ cup stoned black olives
    (about 12)
salt and freshly ground black pepper

1 To make the stuffing, cook the chopped onion gently in 25 g/1 oz/2 tbsp butter until soft. Turn into a bowl and cool. Add the remaining ingredients, except the rest of the butter, mix thoroughly and season.

2 To bone the chicken, use a small, sharp knife to remove the wing tips (pinions). Turn the chicken over on to its breast and cut a line down the backbone.

3 Cut the flesh away from the carcass, scraping the bones clean. Carefully cut through the sinew around the leg and wing joints and scrape the knife down the bones to free them. Remove the carcass, taking care not to cut through the skin along the breastbone.

4 To stuff the chicken, lay it flat, skin side down, and level the flesh as much as possible. Shape the stuffing down the centre of the chicken and fold the sides over the stuffing. Sew the flesh neatly together, using a needle and dark thread. Tie with fine string into a roll.

5 Preheat the oven to 180°C/350°F/ Gas 4. Place the roll, with the join underneath, on a rack in a roasting tin and brush with the remaining butter. Bake uncovered for 1¼ hours, or until cooked, basting frequently. When cool, remove the string and thread. Wrap in foil and chill until ready to serve or freeze.

COOK'S TIP: Thaw the chicken roll from frozen for 12 hours in the fridge, and leave to stand at cool room temperature for an hour before serving. Use dark thread for sewing, as it is much easier to see when you come to remove it once the roll is cooked.

Chicken Véronique

When grapes are used in any savoury dish, it is often called "Véronique" or sometimes "à la vigneronne" after the wife of the grape grower.

Serves 4

INGREDIENTS
4 boneless chicken breasts (about 200 g/7 oz each), well trimmed
25 g/1 oz/2 tbsp butter
1 large or 2 small shallots, chopped
120 ml/4 fl oz/½ cup dry white wine
250 ml/8 fl oz/1 cup chicken stock
120 ml/4 fl oz/½ cup whipping cream
150 g/5 oz/1 cup (about 30) seedless green grapes
salt and freshly ground black pepper
fresh parsley, to garnish

1 Season the chicken breasts. Melt half the butter in a frying pan over a medium-high heat and cook the chicken breasts for 4–5 minutes on each side, until golden.

2 Transfer the chicken breasts to a plate and cover to keep warm. Add the remaining butter and sauté the shallots until just softened, stirring frequently.

3 Add the wine, bring to the boil and boil to reduce by half, then add the stock and continue boiling to reduce by half again.

4 Add the cream to the sauce, bring back to the boil, and add any juices from the chicken. Add the grapes and cook gently for 5 minutes.

5 Slice the cooked chicken breasts. Pour the sauce over the chicken slices and serve, garnished with sprigs of fresh parsley.

VARIATION: This dish can also be made using a whole chicken, cut into serving pieces and cooked longer. Chopped chicken livers can be lightly stir-fried and added to the sauce with the grapes, if liked.

Chicken en Croûte

Chicken breasts, layered with herbs and orange-flavoured stuffing and wrapped in light puff pastry, make an impressive dish to serve at a dinner party or special occasion.

Serves 8

INGREDIENTS
1 x 450 g/1 lb packet puff pastry
4 large boned and skinned chicken breasts
1 egg, beaten

FOR THE STUFFING
115 g/4 oz leeks, thinly sliced
50 g/2 oz streaky bacon, chopped
25 g/1 oz/2 tbsp butter
115 g/4 oz/2 cups fresh white breadcrumbs
30 ml/2 tbsp chopped fresh herbs, e.g.
   parsley, thyme, marjoram and chives
grated rind of 1 large orange
1 egg, beaten
orange juice or stock (optional)
salt and freshly ground black pepper

1 First make the stuffing. Cook the leeks and bacon in the butter until soft. Put the breadcrumbs into a bowl with the herbs and plenty of seasoning. Add the leeks, bacon and butter with the grated orange rind and bind with the beaten egg. If the mixture is too dry and crumbly, add a little orange juice or stock.

2 Roll the pastry out to a rectangle 30 x 40 cm/12 x 16 in. Trim the edges and reserve for the decoration. Preheat the oven to 200°C/400°F/ Gas 6. Grease a baking tray.

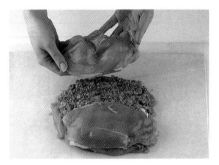

3 Place the boned chicken breasts between two pieces of clear film and flatten to a thickness of 5 mm/¼ in with a rolling pin. Spread a third of the stuffing over the centre of the pastry. Lay two chicken breasts side-by-side over the stuffing. Cover with another third of the stuffing, then repeat with the other chicken breasts and the rest of the stuffing.

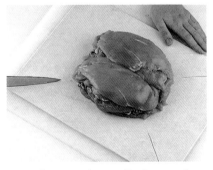

4 Make a cut diagonally from each corner of the pastry to the chicken. Brush the pastry with beaten egg.

5 Bring up the sides and overlap them slightly. Trim away any excess pastry before folding the ends over like a parcel. Turn over on to the baking tray, so that the joins are underneath. Shape the parcel neatly and trim away any excess pastry.

6 With a sharp knife, lightly criss-cross the top of the pastry to make a diamond pattern. Brush with beaten egg and cut leaves from the trimmings to decorate the top. Bake for 50–60 minutes, or until well risen and golden brown on top.

Coq au Vin

This classic dish was originally made with an old rooster, marinated then slowly braised until very tender. White wine may be used instead of red – as in Alsace, where the local Riesling is used.

Serves 4

INGREDIENTS

1.5–1.75 kg/3½–4 lb chicken,
   cut in pieces
25 ml/1½ tbsp olive oil
225 g/8 oz baby onions
15 g/½ oz/1 tbsp butter
225 g/8 oz mushrooms,
   quartered if large
30 ml/2 tbsp plain flour
750 ml/1¼ pints/3 cups dry red wine
250 ml/8 fl oz/1 cup chicken stock,
   or more to cover
bouquet garni
salt and freshly ground black pepper

1 Season the chicken pieces with salt and pepper. Put them in a large, heavy frying pan, skin side down, and cook over a medium-high heat for 10–12 minutes, or until golden brown. Transfer to a plate.

2 Meanwhile, heat the oil in a large flameproof casserole over a medium–low heat, add the onions, cover and cook until evenly browned, stirring frequently.

3 In a heavy frying pan, melt the butter over a medium heat and sauté the mushrooms, stirring, until golden brown.

4 Sprinkle the onions with flour and cook for 2 minutes, stirring frequently, then add the wine and boil for 1 minute, stirring.

5 Add the chicken, mushrooms, stock and bouquet garni. Bring to the boil, reduce the heat to very low, cover and simmer for 45–50 minutes, until the chicken is tender and the juices run clear when the thickest part of the meat is pierced with a knife.

6 Using tongs or a slotted spoon, transfer the chicken and vegetables to a plate. Strain the cooking liquid, skim off the fat and return to the pan. Boil the liquid until it has reduced by about one third, then return the chicken and vegetables to the casserole and simmer for 3–4 minutes to heat through before serving.

Tarragon Chicken with Caramelized Onions

Served with slivers of herb and orange butter, this makes a meal fit for any special occasion.

Serves 4

INGREDIENTS
4 skinless, boneless chicken breasts, about 175 g/6 oz each
2 onions, thinly sliced
2 garlic cloves, crushed
60 ml/4 tbsp chopped fresh tarragon
juice of 2 oranges
45 ml/3 tbsp sunflower oil
15 ml/1 tbsp light brown sugar
60 ml/4 tbsp white wine
75 g/3 oz/⅓ cup butter
salt and freshly ground black pepper

FOR THE HERB BUTTER
115 g/4 oz/½ cup butter, softened
60 ml/4 tbsp orange juice
60 ml/4 tbsp chopped fresh tarragon

1 First, make the herb butter. Put the butter in a bowl. Gradually beat in the orange juice, then add the chopped tarragon. Cut a 25 x 20 cm/ 10 x 8 in piece of greaseproof paper. Spoon the herb butter on to the paper in a broad line.

2 Fold the edge of the paper over the butter and pat down lightly. Roll the paper over the butter, squeezing it gently to form a long, even roll.

3 Twist the ends of the paper to form a "cracker", then chill the herb butter until firm.

4 Place the chicken, onions, garlic and half the tarragon in a bowl with the orange juice. Marinate for 4 hours. Remove the chicken from the marinade. Heat 15 ml/1 tbsp oil in a frying pan. Add the onions and marinade. Cover and allow to simmer gently for 15 minutes.

5 Add the sugar to the pan and cook, uncovered, for 15 minutes. Meanwhile, heat the remaining oil in another frying pan and brown the chicken. Lower the heat and cook for 10–12 minutes, turning halfway through. Place the chicken on a serving plate and keep hot.

6 Pour the wine into the pan. Stir well and cook until it has reduced by two thirds. Whisk in small pieces of butter. Add the remaining tarragon. Cook for 2–3 minutes, season and pour over the chicken. Serve topped with slices of herb butter and accompanied by caramelized onions.

Index

This edition published by Hermes House

Hermes House is an imprint of
Anness Publishing Limited
Hermes House, 88–89 Blackfriars Road, London SE1 8HA

Publisher: Joanna Lorenz
Editor: Valerie Ferguson
Series Designer: Bobbie Colgate Stone
Designer: Andrew Heath
Editorial Reader: Hayley Kerr
Production Controller: Joanna King

Recipes contributed by: Alex Barker, Angela Boggiano,
Janet Brinkworth, Kit Chan, Frances Cleary,
Carole Clements, Sarah Edmonds, Joanna Farrow,
Rafi Fernandez, Christine France, Shirley Gill,   Jane
Hartshorn, Judy Jackson, Sue Maggs,
Norma Miller, Anne Sheasby, Liz Trigg, Steven Wheeler,
Elizabeth Wolf-Cohen, Jeni Wright

Photography: William Adams-Lingwood, Karl Adamson,
Edward Allwright, Steve Baxter, James Duncan,
Michelle Garrett, Amanda Heywood, Janine Hosegood,
David Jordan, Don Last, Thomas Odulate

Notes

For all recipes, quantities are given in both metric and
imperial measures and, where appropriate, measures are
also given in standard cups and spoons.
Follow one set, but not a mixture, because they are
not interchangeable.

Standard spoon and cup measures are level.

1 tsp = 5 ml   1 tbsp =15 ml

1 cup = 250 ml/8 fl oz

Australian standard tablespoons are 20 ml.
Australian readers should use 3 tsp in place of 1 tbsp for
measuring small quantities of gelatine, cornflour, salt, etc.

Medium eggs are used unless otherwise stated.

Printed and bound in China